Where Do I Go From Here?

A Practical **"In Your Face"** Guide For Developing A Successful Life & Business Plan!

HENRY L RAMSEY JR.

R4media Publishing, Atlanta, Georgia

R4media, 7214 Agnes St., Pittsburgh PA 15218

Where Do I go From Here?

Original Copyright 2001 by Henry L. Ramsey Jr. All rights reserved.   Updated

Copyright and 3rd Edition Copyright 2023

Printed in the United States of America. No part of this book may be used or reproduced

in any manner Whatsoever without written permission except in the case of brief

quotations embodied in critical articles and reviews. For information address Reprint

Requests, 615 1st Ave #422, Pittsburgh PA 15219.

First Edition Published 2001

1

Where Do I Go From Here? A Success Guide To Business & Life!

Contents

"Along the journey there have been many who have helped me learn, grow, survive, and stay motivated. Completing this book is a testament to all of them.

Where Do I Go From Here? A Success Guide To Business & Life!

What I do, I do for those I love especially my children and I hope this book not only inspires them to reach their dreams but others who read it to do what is needed to succeed in life and business."

Henry Ramsey

Where Do I Go From Here? A Success Guide To Business & Life!

Preface

"Throughout the centuries there were men who took first steps down new roads armed with nothing but their own vision. Their goals differed, but they all had this in common: that the step was first, the road new, the vision unborrowed, and the response they received hatred. The great creators—the thinkers, the artists, the scientists, the inventors—stood alone against the men of their time. Every great new thought was opposed. Every great new invention was denounced. The first motor was considered foolish. The airplane was considered impossible. The power loom was considered vicious. Anesthesia was considered sinful. But the men of unborrowed vision went ahead. They fought, they suffered and they paid. But they won."

- **The Fountainhead**

This book has one goal in mind; to empower you to become a complete person with balance in all the key areas of life so that you can accomplish your goals and achieve business success. You have wanted to start your business for quite some time now and it has never seemed like the right time. Questions like: Can I commit the time needed for success or do we really have the money to start a business right now or is this the right time to take such a huge risk with our future, have paralyzed you. As a result, you have watched years roll by and you are no closer to realizing your dreams than when you first began to dream. This book helps you to understand that there may never be an ideal time to take the risk of starting a business. You will probably never have enough money or time. That, however, is focusing on the negative. Let's focus on what you do have:

- You have a great idea.
- You have a sincere commitment to your family and those you love.
- You have a strong desire for more in and out of life.

Where Do I Go From Here? A Success Guide To Business & Life!

- You have everything it takes for business success.

What you don't have is a plan and direction. This book will give you that plan and the direction you need. You will walk away from this book with a new approach to life and your business. You will no longer have to ask the question…

Where do I go From Here?

The Purpose

Where do I go From Here? A Success Guide To Business & Life!

I wrote this book because life, excuses, and outside forces seemed to be controlling my destiny and those of many others I called friend. The many self-help books available, although inspirational all seemed to lack the practical approach that I and others needed to really break the cycle. I felt a more detailed and honest assessment of my life was needed, so "Where Do I Go From Here?" was written.

It is important to note that this book was written as an "In Your Face, No Excuses" guide to truly seeing and determining where you were and are in life. Where you go after you realize that will be entirely up to you, but you will know.

The Book Serves 3 Purposes:
1. As a guide for the **committed** yet lost or confused who wish to create the plan, they need to achieve true balance in life and success in business.
2. As a wakeup call to the **half-hearted** who thinks they have been on the path but giving it less that the required effort and a partial commitment to doing what it takes to achieve their goals
3. As a wakeup call to the **dreamer** who thinks they want a certain life, but recognizes through the process, they may not really wish to commit to what it takes to achieve the goals they have fantasized about. (And that's ok, it's better to know and begin really enjoying your life than to live in a constant dream world unsatisfied and barely enjoying the moment.)

As the author of this book, it is important for me to state a simple fact of my own

6

Where Do I Go From Here? A Success Guide To Business & Life!

life: I have not lived this book fully since its original writing. It has literally taken 20 plus years to even re-release this book due to procrastination, fear, and just other distractions. So, I don't approach this book with anything other than humility and a desire to share my vision with others in the hopes that someone else who has been non-committal can finally find that inner strength to not only manifest their destiny but do the work required to get there.

Introduction

Where do I go From Here? A Success Guide To Business & Life!
Introduction I: (The Entrepreneurial Spirit)

As we face the many hurdles that life brings it is amazing that some of us decide to place even more obstacles in our path. Starting a business can be the biggest source of frustration that your life will ever know. However, it may also be the only way of achieving the financial independence that you desire. God (your inner light, the universe etc.) has given you the vision. You have the initial desire and the will to work. You know just how successful you will be if you could just get started. You have the idea and you're ready to work, but the question is…
"Where do I go from here?"

We know starting a business requires more than desire and will. It also requires money, a plan, marketing and advertising, an office or storefront, and some technical assistance. Where can you get all these things, and even if you knew where, how are you going to find the money or the time? This book will help! **Where do I go From Here?** Is a guide to starting a business that doesn't forget about your real life. Unlike most business start-up books that just tell you how to write a business plan and direct you to a few help sources, this book will help you create both a business plan and a **Life Plan**.

Writing a business plan is challenging, but without first creating a Life Plan, your business plan will probably be impossible to implement. Most of us are not like a Fortune 500 company that has millions of dollars at our disposal. Instead, we are working from a small budget that is needed to keep our regular lives moving in the right direction. Furthermore, we don't have hundreds of employees at our

8

Where Do I Go From Here? A Success Guide To Business & Life!

disposal to assist us in carrying out our plan. In most cases it is just you. So, when you begin your business, begin with the understanding that a loan or investment **may** be coming, but until it does, you must plan your business around your current circumstances and what you can accomplish daily. If you are currently employed and are starting your business on the side, then it becomes even more critical that your business plan be based on your ability to fit your business into your already hectic schedule. This book will help the full-time employee who is trying to start a business and the part time business owner who is trying to take their business to the next level.

Before writing your business plan we will have to deal with life. This book will help you get all aspects of your life moving in the same direction, thereby, helping you to create a balance between your life and your business. You will remember why you started your business in the first place, and why you must not allow yourself to give up. The business plan will be created after the Life Plan to guarantee the creation of a business plan that is realistic and easy to implement.

Introduction II: (Life Plan Intro)

The biggest hurdle to starting a business is rarely not having a good idea. There are thousands of people out there with great ideas, but having a good idea is not the problem. It's having the time, money, and plan to turn your idea into a profitable venture all while somehow working your current job, being able to invest in your new business while maintaining your current lifestyle, maintaining your spiritual and social relationships, spending quality time with family and friends and staying physically fit.

If this seems like a lot to deal with, you're right. You deal with it every day. On most days you probably don't even take the time to reflect because you're too busy dealing. Then all the sudden you decide to start or grow your business. Sounds good, but with all that is happening in your life, can starting a business

Where Do I Go From Here? A Success Guide To Business & Life!

even be done without a major sacrifice or an even greater risk?

The answer in a word is yes! But not without an excellent business plan and what we call, "A LIFE PLAN". You see, so many people begin a business only to have it dissolve into a what-if before it ever gets off the ground. The Bible says that we should count the costs before we start anything so that when we are half finished, we don't find ourselves not being able to complete the job. In business, we tend to think of costs only in a monetary sense, but as business, *PEOPLE* (with the emphasis on the word *PEOPLE*}, we must realize that there are some other costs that we must consider. And they are: Time spent with family, maintaining our physical wellbeing, our extracurricular activities and social lives and prioritizing our lives in such a way that we can start our new venture, keep our job if we must, and still have time for spiritual growth. If this sounds like it is going to be difficult, it is. Just remember that with God, as in life "All things are possible". We simply must take some time to define our true priorities, eliminate the non-priorities, and do inventory of just where our time is being spent. **After this, assuming that a commitment to your new venture has been made, the rest is simply a matter of time.**

A Life Plan is an approach to life that considers every aspect of every day and every part of you! You see when we try to start a business, sometimes we forget about life. **What is life?** Life is who you are socially, emotionally, spiritually, financially, and physically (or what we call the **Big 5**). We jump in headfirst only to regret the fact that we are now neglecting our children. Or we find out that our budget was already stretched too thin, and we can't really invest in our new venture like we wanted to. We haven't been exercising or eating like we should and, as a result, we can't keep up with the physical demands our new venture is now putting on us. So, along the way we become unbalanced and instead of having all five aspects of life in balance, they are all out of whack.

Where Do I Go From Here? A Success Guide To Business & Life!

Where Do I Go From Here? A Success Guide To Business & Life!

Introduction III: (The Inspiration)

When my son was born, we spent 1 year in Baltimore, MD so that my wife could be closer to her parents, in particularly her mother. Before he was born, we lived in Atlanta, GA and I was in the middle of starting my business, but I felt that it was important for her to feel comfortable since financially we weren't exactly where we wanted to be, and this was our first child. So, against my pride we moved to Baltimore and moved in with her parents. After about a month or two we decided to attend a church called Zion Temple in Havre De' Grace, MD about 45 minutes away from where we lived. We loved the pastor and the only friends we had also attended there, so we suffered through the long Sunday commute each week. While we were there, I had the pleasure of meeting and befriending the brotherhood leader. **He was not only the brotherhood leader, but he was also a deacon, a father of 5 and he had a full-time job.** Even with all this he had a janitorial service on the side.

When we first met, he told me that he really wanted to make his janitorial service his full-time occupation and not just a side business. So, I began to help him market his business and build his brand to help him get his business to the next level. He acquired some contracts and had his business going ok! But he still couldn't get it to that next level. Every month or so we would talk, and he would tell me that he was ready, but there was always something that occupied his time. As you can imagine, a wife and five children can keep you busy enough on their own, and when you add his other responsibilities with his job and the church, he really didn't have a free minute in the day.

So finally, after 5 months of frustration we talked again, and this time I told him something that changed my life (and hopefully his) and became the motivation for this book. I said:

*"With all the things going on in your life, it is impossible for you to stick to a business plan. **What you really need is a LIFE PLAN!** You need a plan that not only takes into consideration your business plans and goals, but your current life's condition. A plan that understands that there will be soccer practice and a football game on the same Saturday you scheduled a golf outing with a potential client. A plan that understands that in two months your youngest daughter will have to get braces at the same time you planned on getting your new $600 floor buffer. A plan that understands that there will be a church conference the 1st weekend in March at the same time your only part time worker has requested that Saturday off for his sister's wedding."*

You see a **LIFE PLAN** for the start-up entrepreneur is essential to getting past a good idea or part time business and turning it into a full-time reality. Each of us must deal with what I call the **BIG 5** (emotions, social life, finances, physical condition, and where you are spiritually). In my friend's life the **BIG 5** were overwhelming him. He couldn't ignore the needs of his children because he loved them. His social life was demanding due the fact that he was a leader in his church, and he needed to show himself friendly. His finances were tapped due the fact that he had five children. Physically he was in good shape, but I am sure that stress was plentiful, and spiritually he wanted to please God so church was one of his primary concerns.

The question becomes how do you balance the **BIG 5** and somehow integrate your new business into your already demanding life? The answer is you create a **LIFE PLAN!** Although he didn't realize it, there was still a lot of room in his life for his new venture. The key was finding it and then integrating it into his daily routine. In the upcoming pages and chapters I will walk you through the process of creating such a plan. A plan that helps you get your business off and running while at the same time helping you to get more out of life. You see a

Where Do I Go From Here? A Success Guide To Business & Life!

great **LIFE PLAN** will guarantee that the **BIG 5** are in action and in balance in your life. Moreover, it will make sure that your new business is started and successful.

As stated earlier in the introduction, this book will help you in creating your business plan and provide you with countless online resources for starting a business. We have created an online resource guide with links to agencies and organizations that can help once you are ready. However, of all the things in this book the greatest tool you will ever utilize will be your **LIFE PLAN**!

Chapter 1

WHAT IS A LIFEPLAN? - "and what can it do for you?"
A LIFE PLAN as stated in the introduction is plan that takes into consideration the **BIG 5**: Which is you (emotionally, socially, financially, physically, and spiritually) before you even begin to plan for your business.

There are many reasons a person can't get their business from an idea or hobby to a full-time reality, but I am convinced that the main reason is life itself. Some might say that if you want it bad enough nothing will stop you. That you would deny yourself of everything to get what you want.

I guarantee these people have nothing else in their lives other than their businesses and they don't have to choose or they choose not to deal with any of the hurdles the **BIG 5** can bring into your life.

This however is not where you are. You must deal with at least one of the **BIG 5** and probably all of them. More importantly, you want to deal with the **BIG 5**. You love your children and if starting or growing your business means putting

Where Do I Go From Here? A Success Guide To Business & Life!

them second then you won't have a business. Sometimes a trip to the club or a girls' night out is the only thing that keeps you from losing it, so completely separating yourself socially can't be considered. You already live paycheck to paycheck, so how can you possibly invest in a business that may or may not succeed. At the end of each day, you are completely drained and barely have enough energy to concentrate on a T.V. show, so how can you come home and spend 2 hours preparing for your business, and, on some Sundays, the church is the only motivation you get, so how can you give up those days to work on your new venture.

The only thing that can help you get your business going and/or growing is a **LIFE PLAN**. So, what is it and how can it help?

Before we define what, a **LIFE PLAN** is, we must first clear up a popular misconception. That is that having your own business is your ultimate goal in life. Your business is **NOT YOUR ULTIMATE GOAL**. It is only a means to an end. Having enough money, or spending more time with your family, or solving a problem you perceive in society are your true goals. The business is simply a means to an end. Let's face it, if I offered you 1 billion dollars you wouldn't keep working and, if you did, it would involve doing something fulfilling. So don't walk into this plan thinking that your ultimate goal is your business, but keep in mind that it may be the only thing that can help get you there.

Up until now, those who consulted start-up entrepreneurs made starting a business like joining the Army. You were told you had to give up everything and be willing to sacrifice anything if you wanted to succeed. Statistics show that 75% of most small businesses fail within the 1st five years, so any educated consultant would draw the conclusion that only the most committed can succeed.

Where Do I Go From Here? A Success Guide To Business & Life!

Well, they're right, but only half right. You see a **LIFE PLAN** does require total commitment, but not just to your business.

It requires a total commitment to your life and the **BIG 5**. For in life, it is the **BIG 5** that truly motivates us to success, and when we forget about the **BIG 5** and only focus on our business, we forget why we are in business in the first place. However, when a man or woman takes out the time to play with their children and hear their dreams, or when they walk hand in hand with a spouse and they share their hearts desires, they then remember why they must push themselves to new limits. **A LIFE PLAN** will not only require you to commit to your business, but to life itself.

With your ultimate goal being balance in the **BIG 5** and a happy life utilizing your business as one of the means to this end, A LIFE PLAN is a guide to self-empowerment, self-improvement and self-awareness. A LIFE PLAN forces you to coordinate and/or re-direct your life to your goals and priorities without neglecting the **BIG 5** and in many cases improving them.

The steps in a LIFE PLAN are what I call the **little 5 (inventory, identify, prioritize, evaluate & plan).** First you must take **inventory** of your current life's circumstances in all areas of the **BIG 5** and record just where you are within each area. Then you must **identify** those things that are positive in your **BIG 5** and those things that are negative. The positive must be improved upon and the negative must be eradicated. Then it asks you to set goals and **prioritize** those goals all while considering how the **BIG 5** might be affected by each goal. After you assess your priorities, you then are asked for an open and honest **evaluation** where you must compare where you are (inventory} versus where you want to be (priorities). Finally, you must **plan**. How do you eradicate the negative and improve the positive in your life and then close the gap from the reality of your

Where Do I Go From Here? A Success Guide To Business & Life!

current life to the future reality of your priorities and your ultimate goal?

Keeping in mind, that your plan must always take into consideration how each activity will affect the **BIG 5**. For if any action is taken that harmfully effects any of the **BIG 5** it will steer you on a path for failure. Note: if you haven't realized it yet, YOU ARE THE **BIG 5**. The **BIG 5** together makes up everything that is you. If you neglect the **BIG 5**, you neglect yourself, and no one can continue to neglect him or herself without it eventually having an adverse effect.

So, this is what a LIFE PLAN is. What it will do for you is quite simple. It will allow you to take an honest look at where you are in life and reevaluate where you want to be. In addition, it will help you create a plan that will get you there. More importantly, a life plan will help you with the most important word you will ever hear as it pertains to self-awareness and goal setting. It will help you be **accountable**! You see accountability is the key to any plan evolving from words on paper to life changing action.

Your LIFE PLAN: once created can make you accountable to yourself and if you have the courage, to others. As you will see in the upcoming chapters, I will lay out a sample LIFE PLAN. You will notice that making such a plan available for all to see will make you vulnerable and open for criticism. It will give critics the chance to emphasize your shortcomings, and if you utterly fail, the world (or at least everyone who reads your plan) will know it.

HOWEVER, it will also motivate you. It will make you ready and responsive. Your husband/wife and children will know just what you want out of life. Ultimately, it will make you accountable. Once it is out there you cannot bring it back!

Where Do I Go From Here? A Success Guide To Business & Life!

All in all, a LIFE PLAN is tool to empower you to a greater awareness of yourself and the better you, all while motivating you to become the better you as soon as possible. The **little 5** will help you achieve your goals and a successful business as long you never forget the **BIG 5**.

Before we begin to dive into the LIFE PLAN, l must make mention of a small but critical point. l wrote this book under the assumption that anyone who buys and reads it is committed to starting or growing a successful business. I assumed that the commitment wasn't a problem, but life was.

The word commitment is thrown around very loosely in today's society. It is used as if to say, "I will, but". True commitment is much deeper than words and even actions. It requires you to invest your whole body and soul. You see some people perform the actions of a plan but never truly put their hearts into it and they never succeed and can't understand why. This is why your vision must come from somewhere deep inside (what I call the GOD part of you). It must be something inside that drives you each day. You see to start your new business and have the discipline to stick to the life plan that this book will help you create, you will have to be truly committed. If not, you will fall short in one or two phases of your plan and eventually your entire plan will crumble along with your business.

A key to committing to your new venture is reminding yourself of your commitment to the **Big 5.** You see, these are the things that drive you. They are where your time and money are spent. They are your life. This venture will improve your relationship within all five areas of the **Big 5** (Spiritually, Financially, Emotionally, Socially and Physically).

*Commit to your venture and stay committed to the **Big 5** and you can't go wrong!*

Where Do I Go From Here? A Success Guide To Business & Life!

Where Do I Go From Here? A Success Guide To Business & Life!

Chapter 2

Create Your Life Plan! – "Planning is critical to success."
Inventory, Identify, Prioritize, Evaluate & Plan (the little 5)

In the next few chapters, I will show you the steps required to create an effective plan. I call these areas, the **little 5** and each area will provide you with an in depth look at your current circumstances and allow you to compare them to your stated goals and priorities.

Having a life plan is essential because it provides direction, purpose, and a sense of control over your life's trajectory. Here are some key reasons why having a life plan is important:

-   **Clarity and Focus:** A life plan helps you clarify your long-term goals and aspirations. It allows you to articulate what you want to achieve, both in the short term and throughout your life. This clarity helps you stay focused on what truly matters to you, reducing the chances of getting distracted by trivial matters.

-   **Setting Priorities:** With a life plan, you can prioritize your goals and activities based on their significance and alignment with your values. This prevents you from spreading yourself too thin and helps you allocate your time and energy more effectively.

-   **Motivation:** Having a well-defined life plan can serve as a source of motivation. When you know what you're working towards, it becomes easier to stay motivated during challenging times. Your plan reminds you

20

Where Do I Go From Here? A Success Guide To Business & Life!

why you're making certain sacrifices or putting in extra effort.

- **Decision Making:** Life is full of choices, and a life plan provides a framework for making decisions. When faced with opportunities or challenges, you can refer to your plan to evaluate whether they align with your long-term objectives.

- **Time Management:** A life plan helps you manage your time more efficiently. By knowing your priorities and goals, you can allocate time to activities that contribute to your overall well-being and growth while reducing time spent on activities that don't align with your plan.

- **Sense of Achievement:** As you accomplish the milestones you've set in your life plan; you'll experience a sense of achievement and progress. This sense of accomplishment can boost your self-esteem and overall satisfaction with life.

- **Reduced Stress:** A life plan can reduce stress by providing a sense of structure and predictability. It minimizes the feeling of being adrift and unsure about your future, which can lead to anxiety and stress.

- **Adaptability:** While having a plan is important, life is also unpredictable. A well-designed life plan includes flexibility to adapt to changing circumstances, allowing you to adjust your goals and strategies as needed.

- **Personal Growth:** A life plan encourages continuous personal growth and development. It pushes you to set challenging goals and to acquire new skills, knowledge, and experiences that contribute to your self-

21

Where Do I Go From Here? A Success Guide To Business & Life!

improvement.

- **Legacy and Fulfillment:** A life plan helps you shape your legacy. It allows you to be intentional about the impact you want to have on the world, whether it's through your relationships, career, or other pursuits, leading to a sense of fulfillment.

Remember that a life plan is a dynamic document that can evolve as you do. It's not about rigidly adhering to a fixed path but rather creating a roadmap that guides you while remaining adaptable to changes and new opportunities.

22

Where Do I Go From Here? A Success Guide To Business & Life!

Chapter 3

Inventory – "We have to see where things are!"

You must capture your current life's circumstances to know just how you are currently handling the **BIG 5** and how far from starting your business you really are.

How are you utilizing your time and your money as they relate to the **BIG 5**?

It was once said that a man's priorities can be measured by his calendar and his checkbook. I believe whole heartedly in this statement. If you really want to know what you value most, just check out where your money and your time are spent. (Example: Your largest single expenditure is probably your rent or mortgage. Why: because the most important thing in life is having a place to lay your head. There is nothing wrong with this being your greatest expenditure, but it clearly illustrates how we prioritize our lives.)

As we look at how our time is spent, we must see just how much time is being spent in the areas of our physical health, financial stability, our emotional stability, our family support, and our social lives. Finally, if God is a part of your life, where and how does he fit? For if you say something is important, but you don't spend any time with it, is it really important?
So, your inventory must be complete with time and money as your catalyst. However, to complete a LIFE PLAN we will have to dig a little deeper than this. So, in addition to completing your Time & Money schedules, you will be asked to address each of the **BIG 5** as they fit in to each day. Often a person will step out to start a business without knowing where they currently stand in life.

Where Do I Go From Here? A Success Guide To Business & Life!

Inventory of your **BIG 5** will insure awareness.

Emotionally:

- Check your schedule to see just how much time is spent on emotional stabilization.
- Are you spending quality time with family?
- Are you expressing yourself to those you love?
- Did you tell your spouse, children, and/or someone you love them today?

Socially:

- Are you spending too much, or too little time involved in social activities?
- Are you involving your loved ones in these activities or are you a loner?

Physically:

- What kind of shape are you in?
- Are you where you really want to be?
- Do you have the energy to go beyond the demands of your day?

Financially:

- Are you living within your means?
- Are you saving enough (10%)?
- Have you begun preparing for your child's college education?
- What are you spending each day, week, and month?

Spiritually:

- When is the last time you prayed?
- When is the last time you went to church, temple, or synagogue?

Where Do I Go From Here? A Success Guide To Business & Life!

- Is your relationship with God in order?
- Is your spirituality active or passive?

In addition to the schedules, you will be required to fill out each day for your inventory, you must also write down where you stand with the **BIG 5** each day.

This process is simple but demands attention to details and complete honesty. Nothing can be left out or embellished if you are to make an honest evaluation later.

To begin, take out a notebook and literally write down what you did every hour of every day for the past 7 days. If there was a major emergency in your life during that time, go back an additional 7 days or start from today.
Don't do anything but write down just what you did. Don't try to make excuses or give reasons, just recapture the moments. In addition, write down 2-3 questions for each of the **BIG 5** that are important in **YOUR LIFE**, and answer those questions each day. After you write everything down and account for every hour then it will be time for evaluation, but not your evaluation. The evaluation will come from this book, and you will have to adjust your life accordingly.

Use the following sample to help you with your **Time Inventory** (use half hours if needed):

Sample **BIG 5** Questions:

Emotionally:
- Did I tell my wife that I loved her today?
- Did I hug my child/children today?
- Did I call my parents and thank them?

Where Do I Go From Here? A Success Guide To Business & Life!

Financially:

- Did make any unnecessary expenditures today?
- Did I pay myself this week?

Socially:

- Were my social activities for true enjoyment or escape?
- Could I have included a loved one in today's activities?

Physically:

- Did I exercise today?
- Did I overeat today?
- Was I physically exhausted at any point today? And when?

Spiritually:

- Did I spend X amount of time with "GOD" today? (You decide on X)
- Did I show kindness to someone else today?
- Could l have helped someone today?

Sample Time Inventory Schedule:

Where Do I Go From Here? A Success Guide To Business & Life!

Time	Sunday	Monday	Tuesday
6:00 am	Sleep	Woke up	Woke up
7:00 am	Woke up, prayer & breakfast	Breakfast, got dressed	Breakfast, got dressed
8:00 am	Showered, did hair, etc...	Commute to work	Commute to work
9:00 am	Prepared for church, got kids dressed	Arrived at work, returned Friday's calls, emails	Arrived at work, returned Monday's calls, emails
10:00 am	Arrive At Church	Monday Meeting	Conference Calls
11:00 am	In Church	15 min. break back to work	
12:00 pm	Church then home to relax	Lunch	Lunch
1:00 pm	Began watching T.V., played with children for 10 minutes, talked to friend on the phone	Started presentation	Completed presentation
2:00 pm	Began preparing Sunday Dinner, took a nap, etc...	Work (browsed internet for 20 minutes)	Presentation review w boss
3:00 pm	Ate dinner with family had family discussion, etc...	15 minute break & more work	Presentation edits
4:00 pm	Began preparing for work, did paperwork, planned Monday's schedule, got kids clothes ready	Work (talked to co-worker for 15 minutes then took 20 minute at desk break)	
5:00 pm	Watched T.V., Cut the grass, cleaned the car, etc...	Finished work began commute home (got pet)	Stayed late for final review
6:00 pm	Talked to kids about homework, did laundry, fixed the dishwasher, cleaned up...	Arrived at home - worked out on treadmill- began preparing dinner or etc...	Began commute home
7:00 pm	T.V., Read,	Church for choir rehearsal	Microwaved leftovers
8:00 pm	Reviewed homework		Ate and relaxed
9:00 pm	Put kids to bed and time w spouse	Commute home 15 minute break, put kids to bed	Prepped kids for bed
10:00 pm	Pray, Read, etc...	Paying household bills, Time w' Spouse, Read	Read
11:00 pm	Bedtime	Bedtime	Bedtime

Please review your chart to be sure that you have accounted for everything you have done over the past 7 days. If the sample items remotely resemble your days, you are not alone. Most of our days are filled with activity, but you will see that you may not be as busy as you might think and there may be time yet for a real go at your venture.

The next step is to repeat the 7-day inventory process only this time you must

Where Do I Go From Here? A Success Guide To Business & Life!

account for every expenditure. Again, if any major emergencies took place in your life, go back 7 days prior. Remember; don't leave anything out, even if it's just 1-dollar it's important.

Expense	Sunday	Expense	Monday
$1.00	Church offering	$2.99	Breakfast sandwich
$45.00	Sunday dinner	$5.00	United Way gift @ work
$5.00	Kids allowance	$7.00	Lunch
$50.00	Cell phone bill	$20.00	School supplies
$75.00	Electric bill	$8.00	Driving range
$150.00	Gas bill	$20.00	Nails for wife
$425.00	**Sunday's Total**	**$62.99**	**Monday's Total**

The 7-day inventory that you create will be extrapolated over an entire month and used as basis for just what we are doing with our money. Now that you have inventoried your time and expenses it's still not time to do anything with this information, we must complete another step first.

Where Do I Go From Here? A Success Guide To Business & Life!

Chapter 4

Identify – "No one can know where they are headed if they don't know exactly where they are."
"Keep the positive throw out the negative!"

This section will be the hardest section you will have to complete. The old expression, admitting you have a problem is the first step to recovery, is how this section can be best summarized. This section will require you to identify the positive things in your **BIG 5** and the negative. The positive will be improved upon, but the negative must be purged or eradicated. The bulk of the things, positive or negative in this section, will come from and within you, the rest will come from outside sources and/or people. Keeping in mind that starting and/or improving your business is your main objective, these things that you identify, must be seen as they affect your business and your ability to commit to it. So, what is the first step in identifying those things in your **BIG 5** that will ultimately help or hinder your progress towards the creation and implementation of your LIFE PLAN?

The first step is breaking down each of the **BIG 5** and with your inventory (Chapter 3) as an aid, create a list of the POSITIVE things in your life.

See the following example:

BIG 5	The POSITIVE Attributes	The IMPACT
Physically	I run an additional ¼ mile each time I run	Have the energy to deal with added stress
Emotionally	I spend 2 hours of quality time with my family daily	Have the support of those you love when times get tight
Socially	Once a month we have a girls' night out	Have the support of those you love when times get tight
Financially	I save 5% of my net income	Have some reserve income to begin investing in your venture
Spiritually	I attend church weekly	Have the support of your church family and/or the Spiritual strength it takes to truly commit when no one else believes

Now your list should be longer than this for each category, but the key is identifying those things that you do each day in the **BIG 5** that have a positive effect on your life and will help your LIFE PLAN be a successful one.

After you write down the positive things in your **BIG5** the next question is how do you improve upon these things? Certain areas may not need improvement. Meaning if you already spend a significant amount of time or money in key areas, then you may be doing what is recommended or required, but only you will know this based upon your own life's circumstances.

Where Do I Go From Here? A Success Guide To Business & Life!

For those things that can be improved your steps to improvement might be something like this:

BIG 5	How To Improve Yourself!	The IMPACT
Physically	Add an additional exercise or increase the number of sets w each workout	Have the energy to deal with added stress
Emotionally	Create quality experiences with loved ones during the week	Feel better internally knowing you are giving your all to those you love
Socially	Create a group chat or text with distant or busy friends	Have the support of those you love when times get tight
Financially	Increase the amount you save to 7%	Have some reserve income to begin investing in your venture
Spiritually	Try daily affirmations that inspire you	Have the ability to remain positive in moments of stress or a lost deal

The key to improvement is not going to be done in words, but in actions. These improvements will eventually become a part of your LIFE PLAN, but for now simply record them as part of the improvement of the positive things in your life.

Your next step is to identify the negative things in your life. What are negative things? These are the things or people that cause you to procrastinate, waste time or money, gain weight, be stressed, worry, etc... The negative things are cancerous. They don't help you; instead, they hinder you.

What are some examples of these things in the **BIG 5**?

BIG 5	The NEGATIVE Attributes	The IMPACT
Physically	I am 20lbs overweight because I rarely workout and eat badly late at night	Have little energy to deal with added stress personally or professionally
Emotionally	I often snap or get snippy with loved ones during stressful times	Loved ones avoid me and thereby leaving me feeling alone during tough times
Socially	I rarely reach out to friends or spend time outside of my family	Limited outside support or external voices to help when family may not be enough
Financially	I have ZERO savings because I spend everything I earn	Have ZERO reserve income to begin investing in your venture
Spiritually	I have no quiet time or time for reflection	No inner strength or voice for guidance

What you will find in most cases is a balance between those things that you do or don't do that typically result in the actions or reactions of one of the other **BIG 5** that you find negative in. In other words, the fact that you don't save often causes you not to be prepared for financial emergencies or even your basic needs. The lack then causes you stress, which manifests itself in an emotional blow out or in isolationism whereby you never spend time with anyone because you are embarrassed by your life's condition. Then you begin to hibernate and overeat, which causes you to gain weight and be more out of shape, therefore you have less energy to spend quality time with family which causes you to feel left out an unappreciated and finally you completely forget about God and his ability to comfort and guide you through the tough times.

How do you fix yourself and these circumstances? You must purge! Purge yourself and plan for change. Using the above example here is how you can fix yourself and wipe out the negative in your life:

BIG 5	How To Improve Yourself!	The IMPACT
Physically	Design a work-out schedule that will help you get in shape and lose weight	Have the energy to deal with added stress
Emotionally	Decide that you will spend quality time with your loved ones no matter what and you will leave your current condition behind	Feel better internally knowing you are giving your all to those you love
Socially	Find a true friend that you can open up to and be ready to listen to when it's her turn	Have someone you can trust and someone who can keep you accountable
Financially	Save money and earn more whenever possible. Perhaps no eating out for a while?	Have some reserve to help minimize stress during financial emergencies
Spiritually	Find a spiritual partner or online speaker that inspires you.	Have the daily or ongoing motivation you need internally to manage stress

The above solutions will give you balance in the **BIG 5**. It will take time, but the results will look very similar to the following.

Because you decided to refocus on your spiritual self, you now have increased motivation and confidence, and the tough times don't seem as daunting. When times of trouble arise, you have peace and patience. You don't begin to panic or worry. Your stress levels are under control, and you don't snap on those you love. After a while your financial house begins to get in order and you can handle those little emergencies without much ado. Because you are more physically fit, your energy levels are higher and your thoughts are clearer late in the day and mapping out a sales strategy is that much easier, so income starts to flow. Because you take time with friends, your relationships begin to improve and now you can even help someone else who is going through similar problems as you were. You are now being a friend when only months ago you needed one

Where Do I Go From Here? A Success Guide To Business & Life!

so desperately.

Once you identify the positive and the negative in your life, you will be able to design solutions that will improve the positive and purge the negative. When the negative comes from outside, you must get rid of it. If a so-called friend is not helping you to become the **YOU**, you want to be, then they are not a true friend, and you really don't need them in your life. "Many people will come into your life, some to stay, some not. All have a purpose, but the purpose is not always pure. Learn from them all, but don't keep the ones who mean to harm you."

(Note: "Friends" may not know they are a cancer, but you do. And when you do, remove them.)

34

Where Do I Go From Here? A Success Guide To Business & Life!

Chapter 5

Prioritize – "Where Do You Want To Be?"
What Are Your Priorities?

This should be the easiest section of your **LIFE PLAN**. We all know or at least we think we know what we want from and out of life. To complete this section, you simply need to write down all the things you want out of life then you must rank or prioritize them.

Be specific. This section will require honesty and a realistic approach. In other words, don't put your business in front of your family if you know that this is either not possible or not your desire. After you complete your priority chart/s, keep them handy as you will need them for your **evaluation** and **plan**.

With your new business venture in mind, you must now take some time to list your priorities. They too must be listed in both time and financial categories. You must decide what things are important to you then rank them in order from 1-10 with 1 being the most important thing to you!

Remember this is not based upon where your time or money is **actually spent,** but where you **would prefer it be spent**.

We have already covered where it is being spent in our inventory (Chapter 3), however, before you rank them, look at your **BIG 5** and decide on your top priorities within each (again, be specific), then create your top 10.
A Sample List might look like this:

Where Do I Go From Here? A Success Guide To Business & Life!

BIG 5	Time Priority	The IMPACT
Physically	Be in good physical condition by working out 3 times each week, Get enough sleep	Improve my energy level and attention span so that I can better utilize the limited time I have to dedicate to my new business. (more efficient use of time)
Emotionally	Spending 1-2 hours each day with loved ones involved in a communicative event	Strengthen my bond with those whom I will ask to make the largest sacrifice
Socially	One night out with friends each week	Increase my support structure and outside advice
Financially	Review my budget weekly to make sure that I am sticking to it Saving 10% of my income	Stay on top of my expenditures so that I don't overspend in the wrong areas which will affect my ability to start mv business
Spiritually	Pray 1 hour each day	Spiritual guidance and comfort so that I can make solid decisions

Top 10 (daily to achieve **BIG 5**)

Rank	Time Priority	Rank	Financial Priority
1	Working at my current job	1	Giving to my church (tithes, offering. etc...)
2	Spending time with family	2	Household (rent, food, etc...)
3	Spending time with God	3	Providing extras for my children
4	Starting my new business	4	Starting my new venture
5	Spending time with friends	5	Clothing
6	Spending time at church	6	My social activities
7	Spending time relaxing	7	Eating out
8	Getting my 7-8 hours of	8	Savings
9	Cooking	9	College fund for kids
10	Household Duties (laundry...)	10	Other

The key to establishing your list of priorities is taking an honest look at where you really want your life to be. Remembering that your new venture is simply a

Where Do I Go From Here? A Success Guide To Business & Life!

means to a better end, you will probably want to rank it high, but not so high that you neglect the more important things in your life.

Keep in mind, that if you try to neglect the things that are involved in the **BIG 5**, you will not only be hurting your chances for success, but you might be destroying them. When you consider those things that matter most, it is important that you look at it as if it were a perfect world and you had all the money you could possibly want, then once you are finished, move your current job back up to the number 1 position because that is where it will be until you are full time in your new venture.

Remember that it may not be your priority in terms of enjoyment or self-fulfillment, but if you must spend 8 - 10 hours there each day, it is your number one "Time Priority". So, make the most of it until you can get out.

Keep the above charts handy as you will need them later when you begin to create the **evaluation** and **planning** sections.

Where Do I Go From Here? A Success Guide To Business & Life!

Chapter 6

Evaluation – "Be honest with who and what you are, so that you can become who and what you wish to be."

"Where You Are Versus Where You Want To Be?"

Inventory VS Priorities

This is the section where all the above are put into a clear picture so that you have specific information to create your plan. Without a proper evaluation, your plan will not only be incomplete, but more than likely, not based on reality. Without proper evaluation, your plan will be based on your idealistic view of yourself and your circumstances or worse your negative view of you. You need to be able to see the you, you actually are and the you, you really want to be before you can create a plan that helps you reach your goals.

This section will require some homework. You have already worked hard in creating your inventory, identifying the positive and negative in your life, and prioritizing your time and money.

Now it's time to see just what all this means in terms of your life and your new venture. This section will be both a narrative and a side-by-side comparison of the data already collected. You must see yourself in black and white and in the abstract that only your words can describe.

This section will require you to make a complete and accurate comparison of where you are versus where you want to be. Is your time being spent in the areas where you say your priorities are. Are you spending money on the key areas of your **BIG 5** and top priorities or are you spending it in other places.

Where Do I Go From Here? A Success Guide To Business & Life!

This section will help to answer all these questions and help you adjust your lifestyle to accommodate your priorities. This section is crucial in the implementation of your LIFE PLAN!

The first step is evaluating where you are from a commitment level. In a narrative format, look at your time and financial inventory. Then look at those things you identified in your life as **"negative"**.

Now you must decide just how far you really are from your goals and priorities based upon how you are currently living your life. Then take out a sheet of paper and write down your opinion of yourself in terms of your current circumstances versus your Life's priorities and goals.

If, for instance, you are 40lbs overweight and you spend most of your free time eating, sleeping, and watching television with little or no exercise, it might not be realistic for your evaluation to conclude that you can get back in shape in only 2 or 3 months. 2 or 3 months is more than enough for a committed person, but your circumstances may also require emotional support from a loved one, or a deeper spiritual connection that can allow for more inner motivation and a better self-image. So, for you, it might be more realistic to evaluate yourself as motivationally challenged and you might need to start with simply walking 3 times each week. Then once you have proven that you can commit to that for 30 days or so, now you can increase the intensity of your workouts and plan for a realistic end to your weight problem.

This step in the evaluation process requires realism. This is not to say that it will be impossible to change, instead it says that you are aware of just how far away from your goals you really are, and you are not afraid to admit your

39

Where Do I Go From Here? A Success Guide To Business & Life!

shortcomings, and you are ready to overcome them.

The key to completing this section lies in your ability to evaluate yourself and your ability to commit and stick to your commitment. You and only you will know just how committed you are and can be. Don't allow this book or anyone else to convince you to move too fast or too slow. But please be honest with yourself.

A lack of honest self-assessment will cause you to think you are running full speed ahead when in reality you will be running fool speed ahead.

After you evaluate yourself in each are of the **BIG 5** The next step is to bring out the charts you used for your Time & Financial Inventory. These charts tell you exactly where your time and money are going.
(See Sample Charts Below)

(Time Inventory)

Where Do I Go From Here? A Success Guide To Business & Life!

Time	Monday	Tuesday
6:00 am	Woke up	Woke up
7:00 am	Breakfast, prepared clothes for work, reviewed daily plan	Breakfast, prepared clothes for work, reviewed daily plan
8:00 am	Commute to work	Commute to work
9:00 am	Arrived at work, returned Friday's calls, emails	Arrived at work, returned Monday's calls, emails
10:00 am	Monday Meeting	Conference Calls
11:00 am	15 min. break back to work	
12:00 pm	Lunch	Lunch
1:00 pm	Started presentation	Completed presentation
2:00 pm	Work (browsed internet for 20 minutes)	Presentation review w boss
3:00 pm	15-minute break & more work	Presentation edits
4:00 pm	Work (talked to co-worker for 15 minutes then took 20 minutes at desk break)	"..."
5:00 pm	Finished work began commute home (stopped to get pet)	Stayed late for final review
6:00 pm	Arrived at home - worked out on treadmill- began preparing dinner or etc...	Began commute home
7:00 pm	Church for choir rehearsal	Microwaved leftovers
8:00 pm	"..."	Ate and relaxed
9:00 pm	Commute home 15-minute break before putting kids to bed	Prepped kids for bed
10:00 pm	Paying household bills, Time w' Spouse, Read	Read
11:00 pm	Bedtime	Bedtime

A breakdown of the time chart in our evaluation will show us just how our time is being utilized:

(Time Evaluation)

Where Do I Go From Here? A Success Guide To Business & Life!

Monday		Tuesday	
Useful Time	**Wasted/Available Time**	**Useful Time**	**Wasted/Available Time**
7 hours sleeping	3 hours @ work	7 hours sleeping	3 hours @ work
2 hours commuting	½ hour T.V.	2 hours commuting	3 hours T.V.
5 hours working	1.85 hours unknown	5 hours working	1.85 hours unknown
½hour working out		½hour working out	
½hour with kids		½ hour planning	
1.5 hours in church		½ hour with kids	
½hour homework		½ hour praying	
½hour planning			
½hour budget			
½ hour praying			
18.5 Useful Hours	**5.35 available**	**16 Useful Hours**	**7.75 available**

Repeat for remainder of week!

Averaging the two days in our sample we find that we have a total of 6.55 hours each day of available time. This number will be vitally important in our Planning section.

A sample time evaluation might reveal that you could be spending 2 -3 hours each day preparing for your new venture without it causing you to burn the candle at both ends. Once your evaluation is complete there might be 5 - 7 hours each day or on specific days that are not being used effectively and you could dedicate those hours to more useful endeavors such as your business.

Your time evaluation might also show that too many hours are being spent in nonessential tasks. With a slight change you could even find more hours in the day. *(Example: You currently spend 2 -3 hours each day commuting to and from work. By starting your day 30 minutes earlier and leaving 30 minutes earlier*

Where Do I Go From Here? A Success Guide To Business & Life!

(depending upon traffic patterns) you may be able to trim ½ hour each way off your commute, giving you back an additional hour each day. Or If budget isn't the issue but time is, maybe Instacart is a better way to shop thereby saving you multiple hours a week)

To get your venture up and running, you will have to be creative and re-think how you approach your life. If you think outside the box, you will surprise yourself of just how differently things can be done.

Now we need to do the same thing with our financial inventory. However, before we can begin, we must compare our actual expenditures to our budgeted expenditures. If you don't have a budget, then you will need to set up a budget:

Where Do I Go From Here? A Success Guide To Business & Life!

(See sample below, yours may have different headings)

	Expenses		Income	
Rent	$800	Employment	$3600	
Car Payment	$350	Part Time	$350	
Telephone	$75			
Wi-Fi	$75			
Food	$200			
Credit Cards	$250			
Cable	$76			
Insurances	$300			
Gas	$150			
Loans	$225			
Misc.	$120			
Clothing	$100			
Charitable Giving	$400			
Sub Total	$3121.00		$3950.00	
Net Disposable		Less Savings	$360.00	
Total				
Monthly Available For Venture:			**$469.00**	

After we have a useful budget, we can now look at our financial inventory to decide if we are sticking to our budget and decide what areas we need to adjust:

Expense	Sunday	Expense	Monday
$1.00	Church offering	$2.99	Breakfast sandwich
$45.00	Sunday dinner	$5.00	United Way gift @ work
$5.00	Kids allowance	$7.00	Lunch
$50.00	Cell phone bill	$20.00	School supplies
$75.00	Electric bill	$8.00	Driving range
$150.00	Gas bill	$20.00	Nails for wife
$425.00	**Sunday's Total**	**$62.99**	**Monday's Total**

What we will be able to discover is just how much we are spending versus what

Where Do I Go From Here? A Success Guide To Business & Life!

are budgeted amounts are.

- Are our miscellaneous expenses too large?
- Are we spending too much eating out?
- Are our bills more or less than we budgeted?

You may even have to go back and look at previous month's bills to get a better average of your expenses. In our planning section we will have a completed financial inventory as an example of your real expenditures versus your budgeted amounts.

A sample financial evaluation may look something like this:
You may find that each week you are spending $50 eating out which is costing you approximately $200 each month. Your budget only calls for a total food budget of $200, which means that whatever your grocery bill is, you are exceeding your budget by that amount. This behavior will eat into your savings and leave you with no disposable income after your fixed expenses.

You may also find that you budgeted $100 for the cell bills, but your kids' game charges are pushing your bill to $125 per month. To fix this you can adjust your budget by simply limiting their downloads per month. Other changes might include saving more, getting a part-time job or side hustle, packing a lunch, and never eating out or paying off credit cards.

In any case, once you decide on the amount you will need to start your new business, you will need to make budgetary adjustments to get to that number.

After evaluating yourself in narrative, then side by side using your earlier created charts you will have part of the ammunition you need to begin developing your Plan.

Where Do I Go From Here? A Success Guide To Business & Life!

The rest of what you will need to complete your evaluation is nothing you can put in a chart or on a piece of paper. This part of the evaluation requires some introspection.

You must go deeper.

The Evaluation phase up until now only included a cursory surface look at what you are doing with your time and money. This surface look can give you some insight into your character and your true desires or it can show you just how out of character you have been.

Now you must look at the **BIG 5** and decide that even if you are spending the time and money on your priority areas, are you truly committed to these areas. In other words, is your heart in these priorities or are you just giving them lip service.

For example: You may find, through your inventory and evaluation, that you are spending at least an hour day with your family. On the surface this seems like you are really committed to the emotional strength of your **BIG 5**, but with real introspection, you may find that during most of that time you are distracted by outside stresses or circumstances, and you are not truly sharing yourself with those you love (present but not there).

This introspection of your Evaluation is something that this book can only make you aware of, but it is ultimately up to you to do something about it. Furthermore, if through some real introspection you find yourself falling short in key areas of the **BIG 5**, even though your time and money appear to be going to these categories, you still may need to plan as if you have been completely

Where Do I Go From Here? A Success Guide To Business & Life!

neglecting these areas.

47

Where Do I Go From Here? A Success Guide To Business & Life!

Chapter 7

Plan – "Create a realistic daily plan that will bring you closer to your goals with every passing moment."

The Planning Phase - "A Daily Plan To Reach Your Goals"

The best way to start this chapter is to begin with some real insight into just how your daily plan should be approached. I know that after all that you have just accomplished, you are ready to dive right in, but not so fast. Depending upon your evaluation, you may need to begin with small challenges and successes before you create your final daily plan. What does that mean?

If your spending is very out of control, and you have never operated with a budget, then you may need to create a mini budget that only involves food. Set a food budget for 30 days and when you stick to it, it will become a small success. If your time is being spent everywhere other than with your family, you may need to set your schedule to spend 1 hour each day of quality time with your family. After you have accomplished this for 30 days then you will have achieved a small success.

The type of small challenge you set for yourself (if any) is entirely based upon your self-evaluation. You and only you will know just how far off from your priorities and goals you really are. Now you could be far off, but your commitment could be so high that you can dive right into a full-fledged daily plan and succeed at it, but typically the worse you handle your current life, the longer it will take you to really commit to a full daily plan.

Where Do I Go From Here? A Success Guide To Business & Life!

In life, we need to build up to things. From a physical standpoint this can be illustrated, by my own experiences. As an ex-athlete I always think that I can get back into shape in no time flat, so after allowing myself to get 30lbs over my ideal weight. I decided that I was going to get back in shape, and instead of being smart and simply running a mile or so that first day and beginning to stretch and prepare myself for a long recovery, I wanted a quick fix. The first day out I ran about 2 miles. I felt good. I even found myself thinking that I wasn't as bad off as I thought. Well, the next day I could barely walk. Now, because I was semi-committed to recovery, I didn't want to quit, but I couldn't run. So, the next day I could only jump rope. As a matter of fact, the next 2 days I could only jump rope. On the third day I cut my run down to less than 1 mile realizing that I may need to slow down a bit. I did this for an entire week. I felt good about myself. Well after a week I realized that I hadn't lost a single pound. Although I was disappointed, I didn't quit. After ten days, I realized that my endurance wasn't noticeably improving and my weight wasn't dropping, then without thought or decision, I quit. The problem was, I wasn't honest with where I was physically, and I pumped myself up to change where I thought I was. When I reached a point of testing and realized that a longer and harder commitment was ahead of me and little progress was being made, I quit. I never committed myself to the process. It took me 7 years to gain this weight, but I wanted to lose it in 7 days.

This approach doesn't work physically, and it won't work for your daily plan. The worse your current condition is within the **BIG 5** the longer it will take to begin to see results from them. If you have neglected your children for years, one trip to the movies isn't going to cause them to run to you when they are scared. It is going to take weeks and months of quality time before your place is restored. More importantly, you need to know that you can change and commit. For you to have faith in yourself, you may need to begin with what they call baby

49

Where Do I Go From Here? A Success Guide To Business & Life!

steps.

Challenge yourself with small tests and as you overcome them increase their level until you find yourself ready to start your daily plan.

Ready To Commit?

Once you are ready to fully commit, then it's time to begin creating your daily plan. To tell you what a daily plan is and how to create one, I thought the best approach would be simply to show you a sample.

As you look at the sample daily plan and the process leading up to it you will find many similarities between those in the sample and in your life. Many like you, have a dream for more in life without a complete idea of how to get there. The one thing I do know is that it is up to you. I hope that the sample daily plan will help you create and develop your own.

I also hope that you are not afraid to be accountable to someone else. An accountability partner can be your best resource for growth. For once your plan is put in writing and is made available for others to read, you will never be able to go back. From this day forward you will be open to criticism and questioning.

The following sample was based on my own plan, and I will be accountable to all who read it, but I will also be able to inspire thousands of readers like you to step out in faith and make what you have been inspired to do known to those you love and who love you.

The easiest place to hide is in our own minds, and as long as our visions and dreams remain locked away in our minds we will never have to feel like failures,

Where Do I Go From Here? A Success Guide To Business & Life!

but the second we share them with someone else we are forced to pursue them or forever be remembered as someone who was afraid to go after his/her dreams.

The truth of the matter is our dreams don't begin to come true until they are spoken. Until we speak to them out loud or on paper, they don't become real. In the Bible one of my favorite scriptures can be found in Habukkuk 2:2 "... write the vision, and make it plain upon tables, that he may run that readeth it."

This means that once you make your vision known it can then be put into action and dreams can become reality. Please don't let fear control another day of your life. Have faith in yourself. Have faith in your dreams and have faith in God.

A Sample DAILY PLAN...!

Without rewriting the first 5 chapters of this book I will have to give some insight into the Little 5. I will use a written summary of each, leading to a complete Evaluation. I will also make this a narrative with minimal use of charts until we get into the DAILY PLAN itself.

Sample Inventory:

Time Inventory:

Daily: the bulk of my time is spent at work or on useless or on unproductive tasks. During my free time I often find myself surfing the internet, when I should be engaged in sales activities or other activities to benefit my business. In an average 8–10-hour day I spend 6 hours engaged in work related activities and 1 hour is spent on lunch the other 2-3 hours are wasted or spent commuting to and from work. The remainder of the day is spent cooking, cleaning, time with the family, web browsing for future projects or simply watching T.V. Weekends are

Where Do I Go From Here? A Success Guide To Business & Life!

spent watching T.V., shopping, spending time with family, sleeping and in church on Sundays. On average, 6-10 hours are wasted on Saturdays, and 3-5 hours on Sundays. In total I waste approximately 10-20 hours each week with random time (10-15 hours weekly) being dedicated to things like picking up and dropping off my son at school, spending quality time with family in the evenings and weekends, and golf.

If the following chart were created to gauge my time inventory, would show some serious deficiencies in my use of time:

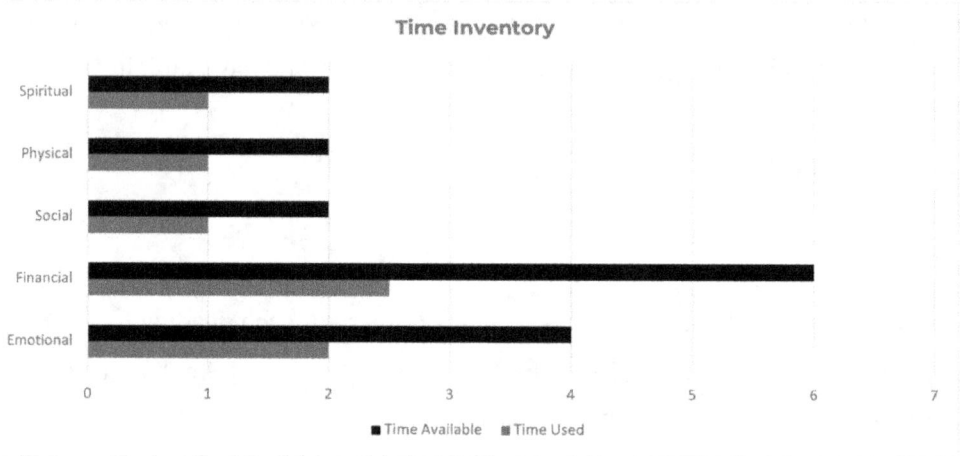

In the key areas of my **BIG 5**, based upon my priorities (financial, emotional, and spiritual) I am wasting more than 5 hours each day. Which means that if I get 8 hours of sleep each night and 2-3 hours commuting, I am only being productive with 8 hours of each day. If this were my actual day I would have to do better or my goal of balance in the **BIG 5** and a successful business would never become a reality.

Financial Inventory:

My finances are also not being handled like someone who is trying to make ends

52

Where Do I Go From Here? A Success Guide To Business & Life!

meet. Instead, I often find myself spending like I have no plans to try to grow my business. We are already operating from an extremely tight budget, so things like eating out and trips to the movies should be kept to an absolute minimum.

As you will see, they are not.

Take a moment to peruse the following sample financial inventory chart and see if there are similar areas where you find yourself wasting money or not spending it wisely:

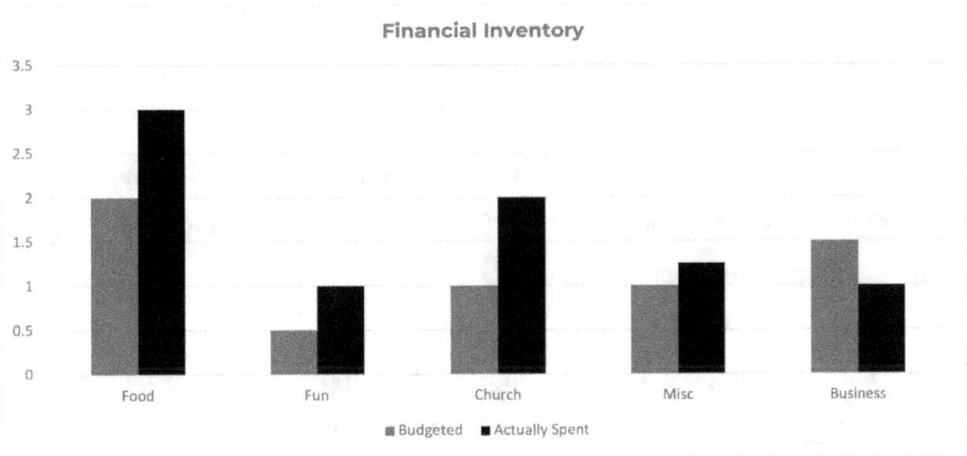

For the purposes of time and clarity I only used non-fixed costs in my summary. Things like rent/mortgage, car payments, insurance, private school, utilities, etc... are what I call fixed costs and there is little you can do to change these amounts without some major changes to your life or lifestyle. If for some reason, you can't find the money you need for your venture in non-fixed costs, you will have to consider adjusting your fixed costs which could mean something as drastic as moving into a smaller home or apartment.

In any case, what you will notice here in my financial inventory analysis is the

Where Do I Go From Here? A Success Guide To Business & Life!

fact that I am grossly over budget in every category except the one where it would be justifiable, my business. Each month I am spending more than $225 more than I should be on non-essential expenditures, and I am spending $175 less than I should be on my business.

By eliminating my overspending, I could easily be able to spend the $200 I have budgeted each month for my business which would be a great help in improving my sales and marketing. However, if I were able to increase my savings to a point where I could eliminate the misc. category, then I would have an additional $125 giving me a total of $325 each month for my business. You may be thinking that $200 or even $325 per month for business is not adequate and for a company with an office and employees, etc... It's not, but for a startup this can help with costs like incorporating, mailings, Google Ads, etc..., this amount would allow me to send out more than 200 targeted mailings each month and attend 2-3 networking events each week.

Your financial inventory may show that you spend too much money on things like golf or eating out for lunch and Sunday dinners. Furthermore, small things like using the wrong ATM machine, or waiting until the last minute to pay a bill and being assessed late fees or having a few too many streaming platform subscriptions all add up to money that could be well spent in other places or simply saved. Remember a penny saved is a penny earned.

Sample Priorities:

As I stated in the **Priority** chapter, this section is what you say you desire your priorities to be and not what they are:

Where Do I Go From Here? A Success Guide To Business & Life!

BIG 5	Time Priority	The IMPACT
Physically	Be in good physical condition by working out 3 times each week, Get enough sleep	Improve my energy level and attention span so that I can better utilize the limited time I have to dedicate to my new business. (more efficient use of time)
Emotionally	Spending 1-2 hours each day with loved ones involved in a communicative event	Strengthen my bond with those whom I will ask to make the largest sacrifice
Socially	One night out with friends each week	Increase my support structure and outside advice
Financially	Review my budget weekly to make sure that I am sticking to it Saving 10% of my income	Stay on top of my expenditures so that I don't overspend in the wrong areas which will affect my ability to start mv business
Spiritually	Pray 1 hour each day	Spiritual guidance and comfort so that I can make solid decisions

Where Do I Go From Here? A Success Guide To Business & Life!

Daily Priorities to Achieve **BIG 5** Priorities & Business Success

Rank	Time Priority
1	Making contacts to secure more clients for Your business (3 hours daily)
2	Spending 1-2 hours with family
3	Spending 1 hour with "God"
4	Spending 5-7 hours on business projects
5	Spending ½ daily communicating with friends
6	Getting 7 hours of sleep
7	Spending time relaxing
8	Helping spouse with 1 household activity daily
9	Giving to someone less fortunate (time or advice etc....)
10	Communicating with extended family on social media

Your time priorities are very personal and how you value them or rank them is as personal as it gets. In my case, my spiritual time commitment is what will help me stay positive, focused, and centered and thereby ensure that my business is successful, we have adequate savings and that our children have money for college. Moreover, time selling is critical to ensuring a steady flow on income to avoid the financial pressures and stress that makes everything else possible.

Your belief system or approach may be different, and you may set your priorities differently. This is completely up to you.

To get to that place in business that you seek, you also must have some very high financial priorities. These priorities must not only be for the immediate needs that you face in business, but the possible unforeseen pitfalls that every family and business must face.

Where Do I Go From Here? A Success Guide To Business & Life!

If you don't set your financial priorities in such a way that you can make the most of today without risking tomorrow, you may not succeed. With these thoughts in mind, I have decided to set our sample financial priorities in the following order:

BIG 5	Financial Priority	The IMPACT
Physically	Budget for better eating habits and save money by not eating so much fast food.	I will stay within my food budget while eating healthier, which will provide me with more energy to promote my business more effectively
Emotionally	Plan to spend more quality time with family engaged in activities that require us to communicate, instead of activities where we appear to be together but there is no communication. (i.e., instead of a trip to the movies which cost more than $30 for a family of 4, we take a trip to the library where we can read together and have discussions)	Reduce expenditures freeing up more money for savings and investment for college and family
Socially	We can take a trip to the library where we can read together and have discussions.	Limiting the number of times out will assist in being at or under budget
Financially	Save 10% of my income	Allow me to eliminate the miscellaneous spending and be prepared for emergencies
Spiritually	Pay tithes & offering	Keep me in line with my beliefs and provide me we with greater favor and benefits later

Now to see how each day will be prioritized & guarantee priorities set in the **BIG 5** are reached.

Rank	Financial Priority
1	Household (rent, food, car, phone etc....)
2	Savings & credit card bills
3	Investing in new venture
4	Charitable giving
5	Providing extras for my children
6	Clothing for family
7	Social activity & fun
8	Helping others

Where Do I Go From Here? A Success Guide To Business & Life!

At first glance the sample daily priorities might seem a little out of order, especially to someone whose business may not be the only source of income. If this is you, simply eliminate those categories and substitute them for your own. In my case, however, the venture is how I feed myself and take care of my family so it must be prioritized.

Now that we have looked at a sample evaluation, it is time to begin creating the actual daily plan.

You have completed the 4 parts of the **little 5** so this part is not that difficult. With all the preliminaries that went into this, you are probably expecting to have to create pie charts, slide presentations, and/or some other major project.

Well, the only thing you will need is a daily planner that comes with some sort of budget tracker. If you use budgeting programs on your personal computer, then you will need to transfer your spending at the end of each day, but that's all.

All the daily plan requires is that you take what you have learned about yourself through **inventory**, **identification**, **prioritizing**, **evaluating**, and **planning**, and create a **DAILY PLAN** that guides you towards your priorities and steers you away from your shortcomings. The two keys to making your daily plan work are:

- Making sure that each day is complete with positive activity that moves you in the direction towards your ultimate goals of balance in the **BIG 5** and growing or starting your new venture.

- *Being accountable to yourself and to others for your **LIFE PLAN**.*

In the earlier sections you created a daily inventory of your time and finances, in

Where Do I Go From Here? A Success Guide To Business & Life!

your daily plan you simply need to take out the same inventory sheet and replace the waste with the productive. Your goal in creating your daily plan will be to improve your use of time, replace wasted time with time spent on your business or on improving the **BIG 5**. This sample plan is only one sample out of thousands of circumstances and no situation will be the same. Let this Plan serve as your guide.

Where Do I Go From Here? A Success Guide To Business & Life!

A Sample Daily Time Plan will look like this:

Time	WITHOUT Daily Plan	WITH Daily Plan
6:00 am	Sleep	Wake up for Prayer (6:00 - 6:15) Shower (6:15 - 6:30) (Attend Leads Groups)
7:00 am	Breakfast, Help prepare children for school	(6:30 - 7:00 exercise) Breakfast, help children prepare for school (Visit Networking Events)
8:00 am	Commute to son's school	Arrive @ school (8- 8:15 commute to work)
9:00 am	Arrived at work, checked email, voicemail, planned for day	(8:45 - 9 check email review daily plan) Begin morning phone calls to prospective clients 9-10
10:00 am	Work	Continue working (take 15 minutes to plan for business)
11:00 am	15 Min. break back to work	Continue working
12:00 pm	Lunch (took 1 hour and 15 minutes)	12:00-12:45 Working Lunch (use time for business calls)
1:00 pm	Late return to work	Return To Work
2:00 pm	@ Work (browsed internet for 20 minutes)	More calls
3:00 pm	15-minute break & more work	Continue working (15-minute break, take notes for business)
4:00 pm	Finished working,	Continue working
5:00 pm	Began commute home	Begin Commute (use time in car to record ideas for business on tape recorder) (Business Calls)
6:00 pm	Began eating or preparing dinner or etc...	Eating as a family
7:00 pm	TV	Quality time with kids" (Networking Events)
8:00 pm	TV	Relax· (Plan for business)
9:00 pm	Browsed web, checked email, some client work	Prepare daily plan for business (Mailings)
10:00 pm	TV	Quality time w' wife*
11:00 pm	Pray, read, bedtime	Pray, read, bedtime

You will accomplish 3 times more for your business within a workday as well as improve the time you spend with your family.

Please note: If you have a full-time job, the 3-1/2 hours that are available to you with the kids, your wife and relaxing may have to be cut in half and then devoted

Where Do I Go From Here? A Success Guide To Business & Life!

to your business. You may have to also spend some working lunches on your new venture in the areas of planning, selling, and or research. You may also consider sacrificing a ½ hour of sleep to devote more time to your new venture thereby waking up at 5:30. Another change may include utilizing your weekends for marketing & networking. Those of you who are already full time in your business, you will have to have even greater discipline and cannot allow the perception of freedom to distract you from being accountable to yourself and your business. Your schedule will need to be even more detailed than that of the person with the full-time job as you will have more opportunity to procrastinate.

In the same vein as your daily time plan, you will need to create a daily financial plan. This plan must take into consideration your average daily expenditures on non-fixed costs. Please think about things like eating out, social activities, and other places where you spend regularly. You will then need to evaluate and adjust your financial situation:

Please try to make adequate sacrifices without being unrealistic. Remember the only way this will be effective is if you are realistic and make decisions that you can stick to.

Where Do I Go From Here? A Success Guide To Business & Life!

A Sample Daily Financial Plan will look like this:

Avg Daily Expense	Without Daily Plan	Avg Daily Expense	With Daily Plan	DAILY Savings	Monthly Totals
$5.00	Eating Out	$1.50	Food From Home	$3.50	$105.00
$1.66	Fun	$.83	Fun	$.83	24.9
$11.66	Gas	$9.73	Gas	$1.93	57.90
$4.16	Misc.	$2.08	Savings	$2.08	62.40
$25.78	Monthly Total	$19.30	Savings	$8.34	$250.20

To realize these types of savings, some action will have to be undertaken:
- NO EATING OUT FOR LUNCH
- COMBINING ERRANDS TO REDUCE DRIVING TIME
- DOWNLOADING A MOVIE INSTEAD OF GOING TO THE MOVIES
- AVOIDING THE VENDING MACHINE AT WORK

You will now have an additional $250 available each month to invest in your business. Depending upon your budget I am sure that you can find similar results by adjusting your spending. Keep in mind, that with the improvements in your work schedule, your income will also increase, thereby giving you more disposable income, which will give you even more money to invest in your business and **BIG 5**.

The key to making sure that you stay on top of your time and your budget is simply to have a daily planner or iPhone® and **USE IT**. You will also need to have a place to literally record every expenditure. I know that this may seem like a little much, but it is the little expenditures that add up to substantial amounts at the end of each month that ruin a budget. One approach that has worked for

62

some people, is to take out, in cash, the amount budgeted for non-fixed expenses. Then once this amount is gone, it's gone. You must be very disciplined to do this. If not, you will not only spend all the cash, but you may find yourself dipping into your budget for more non-fixed expenses.

As you improve your business and your spending habits, you will find yourself with more disposable income. Once your level of disposable income is adequate, you may consider opening a separate account for non-fixed expenses and set a separate budget for that account. Soon you will find yourself with extra money in that account that can be transferred to savings or increased investments in your business.

Your daily financial plan along with your daily time plan will practically guarantee that you stay focused on your goals and begin to improve the **BIG 5** and your new venture. Your daily plan is the most crucial step in your new life for achieving success. If you allow yourself to revert to old ways and forget about the daily plan you have just created, all the hard work you did to complete your **LIFE PLAN** will be wasted and you will wake up months or even years from now in the same position. You will still be living in hope or hoping your business could grow.

You have the power to change yourself and your circumstances. You have just created your **LIFE PLAN**. Through your Inventory you see your current condition. By Identifying the Positive & Negative in your life you are ready to improve yourself by doing more of the positive and purging the negative. You have set your Priorities and Goals and you now know just where you are heading. Your Evaluation has shown you just what you need to do and the sacrifices you will have to make to reach your goals and close the gap between where you are and where you want to be.

Where Do I Go From Here? A Success Guide To Business & Life!

Finally, you created a Daily Plan that is realistic and easy to follow that will start you on the path to true success in all areas of your **BIG 5** and get your business started or to the next level. All in all, you are poised to begin moving full speed ahead with your business. The only thing left to do now is to create a plan for your business.

The next chapters of this book will help you with this process and will show you just what a business plan is and how to create one.

(YOUR LIFE PLAN CAN SAVE YOUR LIFE AND YOUR BUSINESS PLAN WILL REWARD YOUR HARD WORK!)

Chapter 8

Accountability – "An Accountability Partner, may be what you need!"

Staying accountable to your life plan can be challenging, but with the right strategies and mindset, you can increase your chances of success. Here's some steps to help you stay accountable:

- **Set Clear Goals:** Start by defining specific, measurable, achievable, relevant, and time-bound (SMART) goals for your life plan. Having clear goals gives you a roadmap to follow and makes it easier to track your progress.

- **Break Down Goals:** Divide your larger goals into smaller, manageable tasks or milestones. This prevents feeling overwhelmed and allows you to focus on one step at a time.

- **Create a Plan:** Develop a detailed plan outlining how you will achieve each goal. Include action steps, deadlines, resources needed, and potential challenges you might face.

- **Use a Planner or Calendar:** Use a physical planner, digital calendar, or task management app to schedule your tasks and deadlines. Set reminders to keep yourself on track.

- **Visual Reminders:** Post your goals and plans somewhere visible, like on your fridge, workspace, or as your phone's wallpaper. Regularly seeing your objectives will reinforce your commitment.

- **Accountability Partner:** Find a friend, family member, mentor, or coach who can hold you accountable. Share your goals and progress with them, and schedule regular check-ins to discuss your achievements and challenges.

- **Track Progress:** Regularly assess your progress against your plan. Celebrate your successes and adjust your approach if you're falling behind. Tracking your progress helps you stay motivated and make necessary adjustments. (We will be implementing an online CRM that subscribers can use to budget and track their progress)

- **Use Rewards and Consequences:** Set up rewards for achieving milestones or completing tasks. Conversely, establish consequences for not following through. These incentives can provide additional

Where Do I Go From Here? A Success Guide To Business & Life!

motivation.

- **Practice Self-Discipline:** Cultivate self-discipline by staying focused on your goals, managing distractions, and resisting the urge to procrastinate. Develop healthy habits that align with your life plan.

- **Review and Adjust:** Regularly review your life plan to ensure it's still relevant and aligned with your values and aspirations. Life circumstances can change, so be willing to adapt your plan as needed.

- **Reflect on Your Why:** Revisit the reasons why you set these goals in the first place. Connecting with your deeper motivations can reignite your determination. The **BIG 5** must always be in the forefront of your mind.

- **Use Technology:** Utilize apps and tools designed for goal tracking and habit formation. There are many apps available that can help you set reminders, track progress, and stay accountable.

- **Practice Patience and Perseverance:** Staying accountable to your life plan is a journey that requires time and effort. Be patient with yourself, and don't get discouraged by setbacks.

- **Visualize Success:** Regularly imagine yourself achieving your goals. Visualization can help reinforce your commitment and make your goals feel more attainable.

66

Where Do I Go From Here? A Success Guide To Business & Life!

- **Review and Reflect:** Set aside time periodically to review your progress, reflect on what's working and what's not, and adjust your strategies accordingly.

Remember that accountability is a continuous process that requires dedication, self-awareness, and consistent effort. By implementing these strategies and maintaining a positive mindset, you'll be better equipped to stay accountable to your life plan and achieve your goals.

Chapter 9

Rewards & Consequences – "Celebrate along the way"

Using rewards and consequences effectively can be a powerful way to motivate yourself and stay on track to complete your life plan. Here's some steps on how to incorporate rewards and consequences into your life plan:

- **Identify Milestones:** Identify key milestones along the way to achieving your goals. These milestones serve as checkpoints to track your progress.

- **Assign Rewards:** Determine what rewards would motivate you and make achieving those milestones more enjoyable. Rewards can be both big and small, ranging from a treat like your favorite dessert to a weekend getaway. Align the rewards with the significance of the milestone to keep the motivation high.

Where Do I Go From Here? A Success Guide To Business & Life!

- **Set Up a Reward System:** Create a structured reward system that outlines which milestones warrant which rewards. Having a predefined system helps maintain consistency and clarity.

- **Create a Consequence Framework:** Establish consequences that would help deter you from deviating from your life plan. Consequences should be meaningful but not overly punitive. They could involve giving up something enjoyable or dedicating extra effort to get back on track. (No dessert this week!)

- **Track Your Progress:** Regularly track your progress toward your goals and milestones. Use a journal, planner, or digital tools to monitor your achievements. (We will be implementing an online CRM that subscribers can use to budget and track their progress)

- **Celebrate Achievements:** When you reach a milestone, celebrate it! Enjoy the rewards you've set for yourself to acknowledge your hard work and dedication.

- **Address Setbacks:** If you encounter setbacks or struggles, focus on the consequences you've established. They can help you refocus and get back on track more quickly.

- **Adjust as Needed:** Life is dynamic, and circumstances may change. Be open to adjusting your rewards and consequences over time to better align with your evolving priorities and goals.

- **Stay Flexible:** While rewards and consequences are tools to help you stay on track, it's important to maintain a flexible mindset.

Where Do I Go From Here? A Success Guide To Business & Life!

Sometimes circumstances change, and you may need to adapt your approach.

Remember, the key to success is consistency and self-awareness. Continuously assess what motivates you and adjust your reward and consequence system accordingly. By integrating these strategies into your life plan, you can enhance your motivation, stay focused, and increase your chances of achieving your goals.

Chapter 10

Avoid False Choices – "There is always another way!"

Avoiding false choices when planning our lives involves critical thinking, self-awareness, and a strategic approach to decision-making. Here are some steps to help you navigate these choices:

- **Define Your Values and Goals:** Start by clarifying your core values and long-term goals. Understand what truly matters to you, both in the short term and in the big picture. This foundation will guide your decision-making process. The **little 5** should and your priority and goals should be printed and kept close.

- **Challenge Dichotomous Thinking:** False choices often arise from thinking in black-and-white terms. Instead of seeing choices as either/or, consider the possibility of finding middle ground or alternative solutions that align with your values and goals.

- **Gather Information:** Make informed decisions by collecting

69

Where Do I Go From Here? A Success Guide To Business & Life!

relevant information. Research your options thoroughly to understand potential outcomes, advantages, and drawbacks. This will help you see beyond the immediate options and consider a wider range of possibilities.

- **Consider Trade-offs:** Recognize that most decisions involve trade-offs. Consider what you might be giving up or sacrificing in exchange for choosing one path over another. Prioritize the factors that align with your values and goals.

- **Prioritize Flexibility:** Life is unpredictable, so aim for flexibility in your plans. Instead of rigidly committing to one path, create adaptable strategies that can accommodate changes and unforeseen circumstances. For those with families, many of the plans you implement will change regularly, so please be ready to adjust frequently.

- **Seek Diverse Perspectives:** Engage with people who have different viewpoints and experiences. Discussing your options with others can provide valuable insights and help you see beyond your own biases.

- **Reflect on Your Motivations:** Understand the motivations behind your choices. Are you making decisions based on societal pressures, fear, or the expectations of others? By examining your motivations, you can make choices that are more authentic and aligned with your true desires.

- **Embrace Experimentation:** Life is a journey of learning and

Where Do I Go From Here? A Success Guide To Business & Life!

growth. Instead of feeling pressured to make the perfect choice from the start, embrace the idea of experimentation. Be open to trying new things and adjusting your plans as you gain experience and insights.

- **Practice Mindfulness:** Mindfulness can help you stay present and make choices that resonate with your inner self. When you're present in the moment, you can make decisions that reflect your current needs and aspirations. If emotional progress is important in your **Big 5**, this is a critical concept to keep in mind.

- **Set Realistic Expectations:** Be aware that life rarely follows a linear path. There will be twists, turns, and unexpected opportunities. Setting realistic expectations and being open to change can help you adapt to different scenarios.

- **Trust Your Intuition:** While analytical thinking is important, don't discount your intuition. Sometimes your gut feeling can guide you in the right direction, especially when you've done your research and reflection.

- **Review and Adjust:** Regularly review your choices and their outcomes. If something isn't working as planned, be willing to adjust your course. Don't consider adjustments as failures; they are part of the ongoing process of creating a fulfilling life. (Once again, those with families will have to have a living plan in order to stick to it.)

71

Where Do I Go From Here? A Success Guide To Business & Life!

Remember that planning your life is an ongoing process, and there is no one-size-fits-all approach. By combining rational analysis with self-awareness, adaptability, and a willingness to explore different paths, you can navigate the false choices and create a life that aligns with your values and aspirations.

Chapter 11

Why Your Business Plan Is Necessary – "All too often people create a successful plan but fail to follow it."

Why You Need A Business Plan!

As is often the case, when you fail to plan, you plan to fail. No successful business can begin or grow without an adequate business plan. Your business, to begin or grow, needs a quality business plan.

The type of plan you create will be directly related to the current level of your business or the level you intend to begin at. If for instance, you plan on starting a home-based business where you will be the only employee and you will only take on a few clients at a time, then your plan only needs to be created for you and needs to outline those things that you plan to do on a weekly, monthly, and annual basis to get started and keep your business growing.

If, however, you plan on starting a larger venture that will have multiple employees, more than one office, large equipment etc..., then you will need a more professional business plan. One that will be appealing to a lending institution or an investor. This plan will need to be much more detailed than that of a sole proprietor with a small home-based business. I would recommend getting some outside assistance from a professional business consultant or firm for a plan of this magnitude. This guide will, however, give you some major insight into the creation of your business plan no matter what the size. Please use this section as a guide and don't hesitate to utilize the internet or other resources for creating your business plan, as no one outline is perfect.

Where Do I Go From Here? A Success Guide To Business & Life!

Your business may require focus on certain key areas.

The next chapter will provide you with an outline for creating a business plan.

The one thing that I can't emphasize enough is the fact that your plan, however long or detailed, is being created as your guideline for success. For it to work, you must use it. Please don't take days or weeks creating your business plan and then toss it in a drawer never to refer to it again. So many business owners create or even pay for their business plans, then 1 month into the business the plan is collecting dust on a shelf. Remember you are creating this plan because you realize how necessary having a plan is to your success. Don't forget this fact.

More than 75% of all businesses fail within the first 5 years. A major reason for this is the fact that they either don't have a suitable business plan or they simply don't follow it.

Remember your LIFE PLAN has told you where you are and just how much you can give to your business.

You're ready. Now prepare yourself for success by creating and using your business plan.

74

Where Do I Go From Here? A Success Guide To Business & Life!

Chapter 12

What Should Be In Your Business Plan – "Your plan must be complete and realistic"

What's Inside A Business Plan?

(Information Supplied By Strategic Business Planning Co.)

EXECUTIVE SUMMARY (2 -5 pages)
This hard-hitting, concise overview of the business is the last section written... and the first to be read. It must completely captivate the reader, or the rest of the plan will go unread.

VISION AND MISSION (2-4 pages)
This section articulates the organization's v1s1on, or purpose. Of key importance is the mission statement, which expresses the vision as an operational statement that is easily understood and which forms the basis for achievable goals. The goals of the business must be consistent with and supportive of, the organization's mission. The Vision/Mission section links the daily activities of the business to the long-term focus of the organization.

COMPANY PLAN (4-8 pages)
The company must be organized such that it can complete current business activities and those anticipated for the future. The organizational chart should anticipate changes in business size and structure. Strengths of management and key personnel are described in such a way that their capabilities to run the business are evident. Positions are sufficiently described to determine the anticipated salaries required to fill them. Ownership and outside support are also defined.

PRODUCT PLAN (4-10 pages)
The product plan presents a complete description of the product/service and its benefits to customers and other parties. The benefits and weaknesses of the product are described in the most practical, understandable terms possible. The unexploited opportunities that will be (or are being) filled by the company's products and services must be identified in quantifiable terms.

MARKETING ANALYSIS (6-20pages)
The marketing analysis is the detailed description of the available facts and statistics about the environment in which the organization will operate. The size

Where Do I Go From Here? A Success Guide To Business & Life!

of the market and the various market segments are delineated. Growth trends and demographic statistics assist in identifying the actual and prospective markets. Companies with competing and substitute products are carefully analyzed.

Sometimes it is necessary to gather original marketing research such as interviews of prospective customers, either by telephone or by stopping them on the street, to get their reaction to a product. This is usually very expensive and requires a high level of expertise. Original marketing research is usually not essential for developing a good marketing plan (and therefore a good business plan).

It is important to note that frequently, in the process of doing research for the business plan, companies with similar products and/or services are discovered; it usually only takes one such company -- successful or unsuccessful -- to help make decisions for the business that result in savings far more than the price for consulting on the business plan development.

MARKETING PLAN (4-10 pages)
The marketing analysis should naturally lead to the plan for "selling" the business and its products. The marketing plan defines the projected sales in each market segment and the marketing and sales efforts necessary to achieve sales goals. The details of the marketing, advertising and sales strategies should convincingly result in the desired sales and market share. Channels of distribution and methods for pushing and pulling the product through them must be completely presented.

FINANCIAL PLAN (3-10 pages)
The financial plan for the business brings everything together. Typically, investors read this section right after the executive Summary because the Financial Plan expresses in dollars what all the other sections of the plan describe in words. The Financial plan incorporates the cost of bringing the products and services to market that are defined in the Product Plan. It links the acquisition of customers and the resulting sales with the projected sales from the marketing plan.

The financial plan projects all aspects of the organization's financial activity. Usually the financials are month-to-month for the first year and annually for five years. This level of detail conveys to investors that the organization has truly done its homework and gives them a realistic view of the profitability of the business. This section addresses the funding needed and how/when it will be paid back. The financial statements, as well as other supporting documents, are included in an appendix of the supporting documents.

Where Do I Go From Here? A Success Guide To Business & Life!

SUPPORTING DOCUMENTS and FINANCIAL STATEMENTS (10-100 pages)
Organizational Chart Resumes
Financial Statements
Product/Service information
Industry Statistics
Competitive Information
Other Relevant Information

As you can see, there are many aspects to completing a business plan and I would strongly recommend seeking professional assistance before you begin this process. This type of assistance can be expensive, but with the help of this book, you will find many organizations that will help you for free!

Creating the plan is only a portion of the battle, you must now use your plan to run your business, to attract lenders and investors, and to serve as a guide to your business objectives. Creating a business plan only to place it in a drawer will not help you as you start your business.

Where Do I Go From Here? A Success Guide To Business & Life!

Chapter 13

After You Have Planned – "Creating a successful plan is only half the battle, but the war must still be fought."

After The Plan What do I do?

You've gotten the easy part over with. Now it's time to find the Money.

There are many avenues for funding a small business. Each depends on the size of the venture and the credit standing of the entrepreneur. The reason I say that the size of the venture is important, is because there are foundations and other non-profit groups that donate regularly to small ventures ($5000 and under), to help start businesses. To obtain this information all you need to do is turn to the program chart beginning on page 34.

The next avenue for funding deals with your credit standing.

When you have GOOD credit:

The best two financing options are:
- Credit Cards
- Banks, SBA, and other lending institutions

- **Credit Cards:** The best, however, is credit cards. You must search for those with the best interest rates, some as low as 6.9%, but once you find them, not only can you get a better rate than a bank, but you will also always have available credit. In other words, when you repay a bank loan you would have to reapply for another and, depending on your business's current financial outlook, they will

Where Do I Go From Here? A Success Guide To Business & Life!

approve or decline your application. However, with a credit card, if you continue to pay it off, your credit line is always available. Not to mention, if you pay it back soon enough, they'll even increase your limit, and you can avoid interest payments.

- **Banks & Lenders:** Banks are obviously a good source because if you have good credit they do want to lend. The SBA is supposed to be there for all, so everyone should try, but they seem to be difficult for some.

When your credit is not so good, or bad, you may have to go another route:

- Investors
- Savings
- Special lending agencies

- **Investors:** don't have to be a rich uncle or businessperson. Investors can be family or friends. Moreover, to be sure you get to where you're going, borrow a little from everyone you know instead of trying to get a lot from a few. If 20 people invest $500 you have $10,000. Get it!

- **Savings:** is an area that obviously takes time, but so many people fail to realize that putting aside $50-$75 a month in the right place, could have them ready to go in less than 2 years. What am I saying? A lot of people write-out elaborate business plans and they look at these large numbers and think they can't start until they get the entire amount that's written on paper. But what they are

79

Where Do I Go From Here? A Success Guide To Business & Life!

missing, is the fact that they could start on a smaller scale, at home, and build a client base, accumulate some income and re-approach a bank or investor after they've proven themselves, or simply save until they can afford to start. Remember that no matter what you do, time will pass, so you can remain stagnant, or you can try to grow.

- **Special Lending:** includes finance companies who will loan you money at very high interest rates. They usually operate against a car title or a mortgage, or if you work, your job is your security. The interest rates are extremely high, and I would recommend repaying these types of loans as soon as possible.

There are other lending avenues that are available, and I have included their information in the online resource section.

HOW DO I USE THE PLAN & THE MONEY

Starting a business, i.e., writing a business plan, and getting the financing is only the 1st step. Almost 75% of all small businesses started in this country, fail in the 1st (5) years.

WHY?

Once they finish the plan and have the money in the bank, they throw their plans in a drawer, not referring to them to determine how to handle the money or to implement the plan. You see, banks and others spend so much time on business plans, not to see if you know how to write one, but because they assume you will

Where Do I Go From Here? A Success Guide To Business & Life!

use it. How do you use it?

A business plan is your outline for success. Each section must be very detailed. Out of the page or so that you dedicate to a Market Analysis, there should be 5-10 pages on the specific actions that will be made to implement the plan. Every part should have some sort of daily or weekly checklist assigned to it, so that you don't stray from your original plan. If your office hours are stated to be from 9-5, stay from 9-5. If your plan says you will use email to attract business, use email to attract business. Your business plan should be on or near your desk, so that you can check with it regularly. If you get an idea about another marketing tool that's not in your budget, it must replace an existing one (unless you're earning above budget.) If you go off track, get right back on.

Your financial plan is also crucial. It should be updated regularly. Your initial projections will be as accurate as possible, but no financial plan is ever exact in the early phases. At least once a month you should impute actual expenditures, and revenues, re-project and refigure first year's income so that any adjustments can be made before checks start bouncing. If your projection for sales is higher than actual sales, you may want to adjust your workers hours, or their workweek. If you planned on purchasing additional equipment, check the numbers to see where you are before you sink any more money into the business.

Each plan must be followed and adjusted accordingly, and remember you want to be the first to know everything about your business. There is no shame in getting out before you get into debt.

Remember no amount of money will prevent you from failing. You must stay on top of your business. **GOOD LUCK & GOD BLESS!**

Where Do I Go From Here? A Success Guide To Business & Life!

Appendix

From The Author:

I was once told that my greatest attribute was my ability to take many, seemingly unrelated, items and connect them in a way that made sense. When my college advisor (Professor Michael Moore, Bucknell University) told me that, I held on to it. And since that conversation, I have thought of ways to create organizations. companies, groups, etc... that would do just that.

I have worked diligently trying to develop the greatest gift that God has given me, and that is my desire to help others. I have created a company known as r4 media llc. Its sole purpose is to assist would-be entrepreneurs and business owners, in their attempts to start, maintain, or grow a business. This book is the first step.

TO YOU THE ENTREPRENEUR:

My experience in business has taught me that there is no substitute for hard work. Not money, not capital, not anything. For if you don't work at it, the money, the capital, and everything else will be lost.

This book serves as a resource tool for all small businesses who can benefit from these services. The information on each agency is not 100% complete. It has been, instead, summarized for the ease of browsing. My recommendation to you is to find those agencies that fit your company's profile. Then call them to get a full understanding of the services they offer. Every small business owner will at some time be able to utilize this book.

Where Do I Go From Here? A Success Guide To Business & Life!

Online Resources

For those who purchase the guide and share their email address, you will receive a special link to our online community where will gain access to a full list of business and personal resources.

Please visit http://www.wdigfh.com/ to learn more.

84

Where Do I Go From Here? A Success Guide To Business & Life!

Recommended Reading

Here is a list of some highly regarded business planning books: (click to view)

- The Lean Startup, by Eric Ries
  - o This book focuses on the concept of building a business using lean principles, which emphasize iterative development, rapid prototyping, and continuous customer feedback.

- Business Model Generation, by Alexander Osterwalder and Yves Pigneur
  - o This book introduces the Business Model Canvas, a visual framework for developing, describing, and innovating business models.

- Good Strategy Bad Strategy, by Richard Rumelt
  - o The book emphasizes the importance of clear and effective strategic planning, helping business leaders identify and overcome common strategy pitfalls.

- Zero to One, by Peter Thiel
  - o In this book, entrepreneur and investor Peter Thiel discusses the idea of creating and capturing new, unique value in business, rather than copying existing models.

- The Art of Strategy: A Game Theorist's Guide to Success in Business and Life, by Avinash K. Dixit and Barry J. Nalebuff
  - o This book introduces concepts from game theory to business

Where Do I Go From Here? A Success Guide To Business & Life!

strategy, helping readers think strategically and make better decisions.

- Scaling Up: How a Few Companies Make It... and Why the Rest Don't, by Verne Harnish
  - o This book provides a framework for scaling businesses effectively, covering areas like people, strategy, execution, and cash.

- The Business Planning Guide, by David H. Bangs Jr.
  - o For anyone considering venturing into the unknown waters of starting or managing a business, having a voice of experience at hand can mean the difference between a safe journey and shipwreck.

Here is a list of some popular life planning and personal development books: (click to view)

- The 7 Habits of Highly Effective People, by Stephen R. Covey
- Atomic Habits: An Easy & Proven Way to Build Good Habits & Break Bad Ones, by James Clear
- Designing Your Life: How to Build a Well-Lived, Joyful Life, by Bill Burnett and Dave Evans
- The Power of Now: A Guide to Spiritual Enlightenment, by Eckhart Tolle
- Mindset: The New Psychology of Success, by Carol S. Dweck
- Start with Why: How Great Leaders Inspire Everyone to Take Action, by Simon Sinek
- Essentialism: The Disciplined Pursuit of Less, by Greg McKeown

Where Do I Go From Here? A Success Guide To Business & Life!

- Man's Search for Meaning, by Viktor E. Frankl
- The Life-Changing Magic of Tidying Up: The Japanese Art of Decluttering and Organizing, by Marie Kondo
- Deep Work: Rules for Focused Success in a Distracted World, by Cal Newport
- You Are a Badass: How to Stop Doubting Your Greatness and Start Living an Awesome Life, by Jen Sincero
- The Art of Happiness, by Dalai Lama and Howard Cutler
- The Compound Effect: Jumpstart Your Income, Your Life, Your Success, by Darren Hardy

Remember that different books resonate with different people, so it's a good idea to browse through these options, read reviews, and choose the ones that align with your personal and business goals and preferences. Also, keep in mind that the best way to benefit from these books is to not only read them but also apply the principles and practices they discuss to your own life.

References:
Preface Quote: "The Fountainhead, by Ayn Rand – 1943"

87

Where Do I Go From Here? A Success Guide To Business & Life!